PORTUGAL TRAVEL GUIDE

Explore Top Cities In Grand Style From Lisbon, Porto, Sintra to Algarve and discover secret Gems in Portugal.

JULIAD WESS

Copyright © 2023
by
Juliad Wess

All rights reserved. No part of this book may be reproduced or transmitted in any form or by any means, electronic or mechanical, including photocopying, recording, or by any information storage and retrieval system, without permission in writing from the publisher.

Published by [Don Maxwells Publication]

[First Printing: [April 18th, 2023]

Library of Congress Cataloging-in-Publication Data

Juliad Wess
Essential Portugal Travel Guide.

TABLE OF CONTENT

INTRODUCTION
Chapter 1
ABOUT PORTUGAL
WHY VISIT PORTUGAL?:
Chapter 2
GETTING AROUND PORTUGAL
Chapter 3
TOP DESTINATIONS IN PORTUGAL
LISBON: HISTORIC CENTER OF LISBON
Chapter 4
FOOD AND DRINK
TRADITIONAL PORTUGUESE DISHES
WINE REGIONS AND VARIETALS
Chapter 5
CULTURE AND HISTORY
FADO MUSIC AND CULTURE
HISTORY
MUSEUMS AND ART GALLERIES
HISTORICAL SITES AND LANDMARKS
Chapter 6

OUTDOOR ACTIVITIES
SURFING AND BEACHES
HIKING AND NATURE RESERVES
CYCLING TOURS
Chapter 7
PRACTICAL INFORMATION
ACCOMMODATION OPTIONS
LOCAL TRANSPORTATION
LANGUAGE AND CUSTOMS
TRAVEL TIPS AND SAFETY PRECAUTIONS
CONCLUSION
RESOURCES FOR FURTHER INFORMATION

INTRODUCTION

"Portugal Travel Guide" is an indispensable resource for anyone planning to explore this captivating European country. With its rich history, stunning landscapes, and vibrant culture, Portugal has become an increasingly popular destination for travelers from around the world. This comprehensive guidebook provides everything you need to know to make the most of your trip, from practical tips on transportation and accommodations to in-depth information on the country's top attractions, food and drink, and local customs. Whether you're interested in exploring Lisbon's charming neighborhoods, hiking in the rugged hills of the Algarve, or savoring the flavors of traditional Portuguese cuisine, this guidebook will help you plan a truly unforgettable journey. So whether you're a seasoned traveler or planning your first trip to Portugal, this guide is the perfect companion to help you discover all that this fascinating country has to offer.

Than just a traditional guidebook, "Essential Portugal Travel Guide" is a comprehensive resource that covers all aspects of travel to Portugal.

The guidebook includes detailed information on the best time to visit, the country's rich history and cultural heritage, as well as practical advice on local transportation, currency, and language. The authors of this guidebook have extensive experience traveling in Portugal and provide insights and recommendations based on his own personal experiences. The guidebook also features detailed maps, photographs, and illustrations that bring the country to life and help readers navigate its streets and landscapes. Whether you're a budget traveler or looking for luxury experiences, the guidebook has options to suit every style and budget. With its detailed and up-to-date information, "Essential Portugal Travel Guide" is an essential resource for anyone looking to explore this captivating country.

Chapter 1

ABOUT PORTUGAL

Portugal is a country located in southwestern Europe, bordering Spain to the east and the Atlantic Ocean to the west. It is a small country, with an area of just over 92,000 square kilometers, but it has a rich history and culture that stretches back centuries.

Portugal has a population of around 10 million people, with its largest city and capital, Lisbon, accounting for over 2 million of those residents. Portuguese is the official language, and the country's currency is the Euro.

One of Portugal's biggest claims to fame is its long coastline, which stretches for over 800 kilometers along the Atlantic Ocean. This has helped to shape the country's economy and culture, with fishing and seafood playing a big role in the cuisine and lifestyle of many coastal communities.

Portugal has a diverse landscape, ranging from the rugged mountains of the interior to the sunny beaches of the Algarve region in the south. The country is also home to several important rivers, including the Douro, which flows through the historic city of Porto and is famous for its production of port wine.

Portugal has a rich cultural heritage, with many historic sites and landmarks to explore. The country was a major global power in the 15th and 16th centuries, with Portuguese explorers sailing to all corners of the globe in search of new trade routes and territories. This legacy can be seen in many of Portugal's historic buildings and landmarks, including the Belem Tower in Lisbon and the Jeronimos Monastery in Porto.

Today, Portugal is a modern and prosperous country that is a member of the European Union and NATO. It has a high standard of living, a well-developed healthcare system, and a vibrant cultural scene. Its people are friendly and welcoming, and its food and wine are renowned throughout the world.

Portugal is also a popular tourist destination, attracting millions of visitors each year with its sunny beaches, historic cities, and scenic countryside. Some of the most popular destinations include Lisbon, Porto, the Algarve region, the Douro Valley, and the island of Madeira.

In addition to its natural and cultural attractions, Portugal is also known for its vibrant music scene, particularly the traditional music known as fado. This melancholic and soulful style of music is said to have originated in Lisbon in the early 19th century and has since become a beloved symbol of Portuguese culture.

Portugal is also famous for its cuisine, which is known for its fresh seafood, stews, and hearty meat dishes. Some of the most popular dishes include bacalhau (salt cod), cozido (a hearty stew), and francesinha (a sandwich filled with meat, cheese, and sauce). Portuguese wine is also highly regarded, with the country producing a wide range of red, white, and fortified wines.

Despite its many strengths, Portugal faces several challenges, including an aging population, a relatively low birth rate, and economic disparities between urban and rural areas. The country has made progress in recent years, however, with the government implementing a range of policies aimed at boosting economic growth and addressing these challenges.

Overall, Portugal is a fascinating and beautiful country with a rich history and culture. Whether you're interested in exploring its historic landmarks, lounging on its beaches, or sampling its delicious food and wine, there's something for everyone in this enchanting corner of Europe.

WHY VISIT PORTUGAL?

Portugal is a beautiful and diverse country that has a lot to offer for visitors. Here are some reasons why you should consider visiting Portugal:

History and Culture: Portugal has a rich history and culture that is reflected in its architecture, art, and traditions. From the historic neighborhoods of Lisbon to the medieval castles of Sintra and the Roman ruins in the Algarve, Portugal is a country that is steeped in history and culture.

Beaches: Portugal is home to some of the most beautiful beaches in Europe. The Algarve region is particularly famous for its stunning coastline, with its cliffs, coves, and clear waters. The beaches of the Azores and Madeira islands are also worth a visit.

Food and Wine: Portugal is famous for its cuisine, which is based on fresh ingredients and simple, flavorful dishes. Seafood is a particular specialty, with dishes like grilled sardines and octopus salad being among the most popular. Portugal is also famous for its wine, with the Douro Valley being one of the most famous wine regions in the world.

Natural Beauty: Portugal has a stunning natural landscape that ranges from the rolling hills of the Alentejo region to the rugged mountains of the Serra da Estrela. The country is also home to several national parks, including the Peneda-Gerês National Park and the Arrábida Natural Park.

Festivals and Events: Portugal is known for its lively festivals and events, with the Lisbon Carnival, the Festa de São João in Porto, and the Festival do Atlântico in Madeira being among the most popular. The country is also home to several music festivals, including the NOS Alive and the Super Bock Super Rock.

Portugal is a country that offers something for everyone, whether you're interested in history and culture, food and wine, or natural beauty and outdoor activities. With its warm climate, friendly people, and stunning scenery, Portugal is definitely worth a visit.

Chapter 2

GETTING AROUND PORTUGAL

Portugal has a well-developed transportation system that makes it easy to get around the country. Here are some options for getting around Portugal:

Public transportation: Portugal has an extensive network of buses, trains, and metro systems that connect major cities and towns. The national railway company, CP, offers a range of ticket options, including regional, intercity, and international routes. The metro systems in Lisbon and Porto are efficient and convenient for navigating around the cities.

Taxis and ride-hailing apps: Taxis are widely available in Portugal, and ride-hailing apps like Uber and Bolt are also popular. Taxis are metered, and prices are regulated, so you can expect to pay a fair price for your ride.

Car rental: Renting a car is a popular option for exploring Portugal's beautiful countryside and coastline. Most major international car rental companies have offices in Portugal, and prices are reasonable.

Cycling: Portugal is a great destination for cycling enthusiasts. The country has a network of dedicated cycling routes that are well signposted and offer stunning views. You can bring your own bike or rent one from a local rental shop.

Walking: Portugal is a relatively small country, and many of its towns and cities are easy to explore on foot. Walking tours are a great way to see the sights and learn about Portugal's rich history and culture.

Getting around Portugal is easy and affordable, with plenty of transportation options to suit all budgets and preferences.

BEST TIME TO VISIT

Portugal is a beautiful country with a Mediterranean climate that makes it a great destination for travelers throughout the year. However, depending on what you're looking for and what you want to do, some seasons might be better than others. Here are some things to consider when deciding on the best time to visit Portugal:

Summer (June-August): Summer is the high season in Portugal, and for good reason. The weather is warm and sunny, and the beaches are in full swing. However, this also means that prices are higher, and crowds are more significant. If you're planning on visiting Portugal in the summer, make sure to book your accommodations and activities in advance.

Spring (March-May): Spring is a great time to visit Portugal, especially if you're looking to avoid the crowds. The weather is mild, and the flowers are in bloom, making for a beautiful scenery. You can also take advantage of outdoor activities such as hiking and cycling.

Fall (September-November): Fall is another great time to visit Portugal, especially if you're interested in wine. September is the grape harvest season, and many vineyards hold festivals and tastings during this time. The weather is still warm, but the crowds have thinned out, and prices are lower.

Winter (December-February): Portugal is one of the warmest countries in Europe, but the winter months can still be chilly and rainy, especially in the northern regions. However, if you're looking for a winter escape, the Algarve region in the south still has mild temperatures and is a great option.

In conclusion, the best time to visit Portugal really depends on what you're looking for. If you're interested in the beaches and summer activities, then the summer months are ideal. If you're looking to avoid the crowds and take advantage of the spring flowers or fall wine season, then those seasons are your best bet. And if you're looking for a winter escape, the Algarve is the place to be.

Chapter 3

TOP DESTINATIONS IN PORTUGAL

Portugal is a country rich in history, culture, and natural beauty, with plenty of destinations to explore. Some of the top destinations in Portugal include popular cities like Lisbon, Porto, and Faro, as well as picturesque coastal towns like Cascais, Lagos, and Albufeira.

However, there are many other lesser-known destinations in Portugal that are worth visiting, such as the medieval town of Obidos, the university city of Coimbra, the scenic Douro Valley wine region, and the stunning Peneda-Geres National Park.
Portugal is known for its beautiful beaches, and there are many hidden gems along the coastline, such as the Praia da Ursa beach in Sintra, Praia do Tonel in Sagres, and Praia da Rocha in Portimao.
we'll explore some of the top destinations you can visit in grand style on your jour to Portugal.

LISBON: HISTORIC CENTER OF LISBON

The Historic Center of Lisbon is the oldest part of the city and is located in the western part of Portugal. It is also known as the Pombaline Baixa, as it was rebuilt by the Marquis of Pombal after the 1755 earthquake.

The area is characterized by narrow streets, colorful buildings, and stunning architecture. It is home to many historic sites, including the iconic São Jorge Castle, the Se Cathedral, the National Pantheon, and the Carmo Convent.

Other notable landmarks in the Historic Center of Lisbon include the Rossio Square, the Santa Justa Elevator, and the Praça do Comércio, which was once the main gateway to the city and is now a popular tourist spot.

The Historic Center of Lisbon has been designated as a UNESCO World Heritage site due to its rich cultural and historical significance. It is a popular tourist destination, and visitors can enjoy exploring its many museums, galleries, and shops, as well as sampling the city's famous cuisine and wine.
The Historic Center of Lisbon is a vibrant and bustling area, with a mix of historic and modern attractions. Visitors can explore the narrow streets and alleys, which are lined with traditional shops, cafes, and restaurants. The area is also home to many cultural institutions, such as the Lisbon Museum, the National Museum of Contemporary Art, and the National Theater of São Carlos.

One of the most popular attractions in the Historic Center of Lisbon is the Alfama neighborhood. This historic district is characterized by its narrow streets, colorful buildings, and traditional Portuguese architecture. Visitors can explore the area's many shops, cafes, and restaurants, as well as the São Jorge Castle and the Fado Museum.

Another must-visit attraction in the area is the Belem Tower. This iconic tower was built in the early 16th century as a fortress to guard the entrance to Lisbon's harbor. Today, it is one of the most recognizable landmarks in the city and a popular spot for tourists to take photos.

Overall, the Historic Center of Lisbon is a fascinating area to explore, with a rich history and culture that has been preserved for centuries. Whether you are interested in history, architecture, or simply want to experience the vibrant culture of Lisbon, this area has something to offer everyone.

BELEM TOWER AND JERONIMOS MONASTERY

BELEM TOWER

JERONIMOS MONASTERY

The Belem Tower and Jeronimos Monastery are two famous landmarks located in Lisbon, Portugal. Both structures are UNESCO World Heritage Sites and are significant examples of Manueline architecture, a style that emerged in Portugal during the 16th century.

The Belem Tower, also known as the Tower of St. Vincent, was constructed in the early 16th century as a fortress to protect Lisbon's harbor. It features ornate decoration, including maritime motifs, such as ropes and anchors, as well as intricate stone carvings of exotic animals and plants.

The Jeronimos Monastery, also known as the Hieronymites Monastery, was built in the late 15th century by King Manuel I to commemorate Vasco da Gama's successful voyage to India. The monastery features beautiful Manueline architecture, with ornate details such as intricate stone carvings, arches, and vaulted ceilings.

Both structures are important symbols of Portugal's rich history and culture and attract many visitors every year. They are must-see destinations for anyone visiting Lisbon, offering a glimpse into Portugal's glorious past.

The Belem Tower and Jeronimos Monastery are both located in the Belem district of Lisbon, a historic and picturesque area that also features other notable landmarks, such as the Discoveries Monument and the Belem Palace.

The Belem Tower is a five-story structure that stands at the mouth of the Tagus River. It has a pentagonal shape, with each side featuring a different design, reflecting Portugal's exploratory spirit and the cultural exchange that occurred during the Age of Discovery.

The Jeronimos Monastery is a massive complex that includes a church, cloisters, and a grand entrance portal. The church is particularly impressive, featuring a nave that is over 300 feet long, with a vaulted ceiling that is 100 feet high.

Both the Belem Tower and Jeronimos Monastery have undergone extensive restoration work over the years to preserve their architectural and historical significance. Today, they continue to be popular tourist attractions, drawing visitors from all over the world who come to admire their beauty and learn about Portugal's fascinating history.

ALFAMA NEIGHBORHOOD

Alfama is a historic neighborhood in the city of Lisbon, Portugal. It is located on a hill overlooking the Tagus River and is known for its narrow winding streets, colorful buildings, and traditional Portuguese culture.

Alfama is one of the oldest neighborhoods in Lisbon, and it has a rich history that dates back to the Moors and the Roman Empire. The neighborhood has survived numerous earthquakes and fires over the centuries and has managed to retain much of its original character.

Today, Alfama is a popular tourist destination, known for its lively atmosphere and authentic Portuguese cuisine. Visitors can explore the neighborhood on foot, taking in the sights and sounds of the local markets, fado music performances, and traditional cafes.

Some of the popular attractions in Alfama include the Castelo de São Jorge, a medieval castle that offers panoramic views of the city; the Sé de Lisboa, a Romanesque cathedral that dates back to the 12th century; and the National Pantheon, a Baroque church that houses the tombs of many famous Portuguese figures.

Alfama is also known for its vibrant nightlife, with many bars and restaurants staying open late into the night. Overall, Alfama is a charming and picturesque neighborhood that offers visitors a glimpse into Lisbon's rich history and culture

LISBON OCEANARIUM

The Lisbon Oceanarium, also known as the Oceanário de Lisboa, is a large public aquarium located in the Parque das Nações district of Lisbon, Portugal. It is one of the largest indoor aquariums in Europe and is home to a wide variety of marine species from all over the world.

The Oceanarium is divided into four main tanks that represent different ocean habitats: the North Atlantic Tank, the Antarctic Tank, the Pacific Tank, and the Indian Ocean Tank. The tanks are filled with over 7 million liters of saltwater and house a diverse range of marine life, including sharks, rays, sea turtles, octopuses, and many species of fish.

One of the most popular exhibits at the Oceanarium is the Ocean Sunfish, or Mola Mola, which is one of the largest bony fish in the world. Visitors can also see penguins, sea otters, and other sea birds in the outdoor exhibits.

In addition to the exhibits, the Oceanarium offers educational programs and activities for children and adults, including guided tours, workshops, and lectures. It is open daily and attracts over one million visitors each year.

The Lisbon Oceanarium was opened in 1998 as part of the Expo '98 world exposition held in Lisbon. It was designed by the American architect Peter Chermayeff and is considered one of his most significant works. The building's distinctive architecture features a large, curved roof that resembles a wave and is intended to evoke the feeling of being underwater.

The Oceanarium has a strong focus on conservation and education, and works to raise awareness about the importance of protecting marine ecosystems. It is involved in several conservation initiatives, including research projects and breeding programs for endangered species.

One of the Oceanarium's notable breeding programs is for the critically endangered North Atlantic Right Whale, which has been successfully bred in captivity at the facility. The Oceanarium is also involved in research projects studying the effects of climate change on marine ecosystems and the behavior of marine mammals.

The Oceanarium is a popular tourist attraction in Lisbon, and visitors can purchase tickets online or at the entrance. The facility is open year-round, except for Christmas Day, and offers discounted tickets for children, seniors, and groups

PORTO

Porto is a beautiful city located in the northwest of Portugal, on the banks of the Douro River. It is known for its rich history, beautiful architecture, and delicious food and wine.

One of the most famous landmarks in Porto is the Dom Luís I Bridge, which spans the Douro River and offers stunning views of the city. Another notable landmark is the Torre dos Clérigos, a tall bell tower that offers panoramic views of the city from the top.

The historic center of Porto, known as the Ribeira, is a UNESCO World Heritage Site and is home to a number of beautiful buildings and landmarks, including the Palácio da Bolsa, the São Francisco Church, and the Porto Cathedral.

Porto is also known for its delicious food and wine. The city is famous for its port wine, which is produced in the Douro Valley and aged in the wine cellars of Vila Nova de Gaia, across the river from Porto. Visitors can take tours of the port wine cellars and enjoy tastings of the city's most famous export.

In addition to port wine, Porto is also known for its delicious seafood, including fresh fish and shellfish. The city's many restaurants and cafes serve up a variety of traditional Portuguese dishes, as well as international cuisine.

Overall, Porto is a beautiful and historic city that offers something for everyone, from stunning architecture and landmarks to delicious food and wine. It is a must-visit destination for anyone traveling to Portugal.

Porto has a rich cultural scene, with numerous museums, galleries, and theaters. The Serralves Museum of Contemporary Art is a must-see, with its striking modern architecture and impressive collection of contemporary art. The Casa da Música is another iconic building, designed by the Dutch architect Rem Koolhaas, and is home to the Porto Symphony Orchestra.

The city also hosts a number of festivals throughout the year, including the São João Festival, which takes place in June and is known for its lively street parties and traditional celebrations. Another popular festival is the Porto Wine Festival, which takes place in September and celebrates the city's famous port wine.

For those who love the outdoors, Porto is surrounded by beautiful natural landscapes. The Douro Valley, where the port wine is produced, is a stunning area of rolling hills and vineyards, and is easily accessible from the city. The nearby beaches of Matosinhos and Foz do Douro are also popular destinations for swimming, sunbathing, and surfing. In terms of transportation, Porto has a well-developed public transport system, including buses, trams, and metro lines, making it easy to get around the city and explore its many attractions. It is also a great base for exploring other parts of Portugal, with frequent train and bus connections to destinations like Lisbon and the Algarve.

In conclusion, Porto is a vibrant and diverse city with a rich cultural heritage and a lively modern scene. From its stunning architecture and historic landmarks to its delicious food and wine, Porto is a destination that should be on every traveler's bucket list.

RIBEIRA DISTRICT

The Ribeira District, also known as the Ribeira Square or Porto's riverside quarter, is a historic neighborhood in the city of Porto, Portugal. It is located on the banks of the Douro River, and it was declared a UNESCO World Heritage Site in 1996.

The Ribeira District is characterized by its narrow streets, colorful buildings, and lively atmosphere. It is a popular destination for tourists, who can enjoy the area's many cafes, restaurants, and shops, as well as its beautiful views of the river.

Some of the notable landmarks in the Ribeira District include the Ribeira Square, the Ponte Dom Luis I bridge, the Porto Cathedral, and the Palacio da Bolsa. The district is also home to several museums and cultural centers, such as the Museum of Port Wine and the Serralves Foundation.

The Ribeira District is a must-see destination for anyone visiting Porto, and it offers a unique glimpse into the city's rich history and culture

PORT WINE CELLARS

Port Wine Cellars are wine storage facilities located in the Douro Valley region of Portugal, where Port wine is produced. Port wine is a fortified wine, meaning that it is a wine that has had a distilled spirit, typically brandy, added to it. This process stops the fermentation of the wine and leaves it with a higher alcohol content and a sweeter taste.

The Port Wine Cellars are typically located in the city of Vila Nova de Gaia, which is across the river from the city of Porto. This location was chosen because of its proximity to the Douro River, which was historically used to transport the wine barrels from the vineyards in the Douro Valley down to the city.

In the Port Wine Cellars, the wine is aged in oak barrels for several years, during which time it develops its characteristic taste and aroma. The wine is also regularly tasted and blended to ensure that it meets the quality standards of the Port wine industry.

Visitors to the Port Wine Cellars can take guided tours of the facilities and learn about the history and production of Port wine. They can also taste different varieties of Port wine and purchase bottles to take home.

CLERIGOS TOWER

The Clérigos Tower is an iconic landmark located in the city of Porto, Portugal. It is a tall baroque bell tower that was built between 1732 and 1763, and is considered one of the city's most prominent symbols.

The tower was designed by Italian architect Nicolau Nasoni, and stands at 75 meters (246 feet) tall. It has six floors and a total of 225 steps to reach the top, where visitors can enjoy panoramic views of the city.

The Clérigos Tower is part of the Clérigos Church and Museum complex, which includes the church, the museum, and a beautiful baroque-style building. The tower and church were built to serve as a symbol of the city's religious and cultural heritage. Today, the Clérigos Tower is one of the most popular tourist attractions in Porto, and visitors can climb the tower to take in stunning views of the city and the surrounding area.

SERRALVES MUSEUM AND GARDENS

Serralves Museum and Gardens is a contemporary art museum located in Porto, Portugal. It is one of the most important cultural institutions in the country and is known for its modern and contemporary art collections, as well as its beautiful gardens and park.

The museum was designed by the renowned Portuguese architect, Alvaro Siza Vieira, and opened its doors to the public in 1999. It is housed in a distinctive modernist building, which is surrounded by 18 hectares of landscaped gardens, designed by Jacques Gréber.

The museum's collection includes works by some of the most significant artists of the 20th and 21st centuries, such as Francis Bacon, Joan Miró, and Andy Warhol, among others. The museum also hosts temporary exhibitions, performances, and other cultural events throughout the year.

The gardens of Serralves Museum are a must-see attraction for visitors to Porto. They feature a wide range of plant species, including rare and exotic plants, as well as lakes, fountains, and sculptures. The park also has several walking trails, allowing visitors to explore its various areas.

In addition to its artistic and natural attractions, Serralves Museum offers a variety of educational programs for visitors of all ages, including guided tours, workshops, and lectures.

Serralves Museum and Gardens is a must-visit destination for art and nature lovers visiting Porto, and it offers a unique cultural experience that is sure to leave a lasting impression.

SINTRA

Sintra is a town located in the Greater Lisbon region of Portugal, approximately 25 km northwest of Lisbon. It is known for its beautiful historic center, which is a UNESCO World Heritage Site, and its many palaces, estates, and gardens.

One of the most famous landmarks in Sintra is the Palácio Nacional de Sintra, a royal palace that dates back to the 14th century. Other notable attractions include the Moorish Castle, the Pena Palace, and the Quinta da Regaleira estate, which features a palace, chapel, and gardens.

Sintra has a rich cultural history, with influences from the Moors, the Portuguese monarchy, and various other European cultures. Today, it is a popular tourist destination, attracting visitors from around the world who come to explore its stunning architecture, natural beauty, and rich cultural heritage.
As I mentioned earlier, Sintra is a town with a long and fascinating history. It was first settled by the Moors in the 8th century, and later became a favored summer residence of the Portuguese royal family in the 19th century.

One of the most striking features of Sintra is its natural setting. The town is nestled in the foothills of the Serra de Sintra, a mountain range that rises up from the Atlantic coast. The mountainous terrain and lush vegetation give Sintra a uniquely picturesque atmosphere.

In addition to its palaces and estates, Sintra is also home to a number of churches, museums, and cultural institutions. For example, the Museu Anjos Teixeira showcases the work of the artist António Augusto Gonçalves, who was born in Sintra.

Sintra is also known for its traditional cuisine, which features seafood, grilled meats, and pastries such as the famous queijadas de Sintra, a kind of cheese tart. Visitors can sample local specialties at the many restaurants and cafes in the town center.

Sintra is a place of great natural beauty, rich history, and cultural significance. Whether you're interested in exploring its palaces and gardens, learning about its history and culture, or simply enjoying the stunning scenery, Sintra is a must-visit destination in Portugal.

PENA PALACE

Pena Palace is a 19th-century Romanticist castle located in Sintra, Portugal. It is one of the most popular tourist attractions in Portugal and is known for its vibrant colors, unique architecture, and stunning views.

The palace was commissioned by King Ferdinand II and was completed in 1854. It was designed by Baron Wilhelm Ludwig von Eschwege in a Romanticist style that incorporated elements of Gothic, Moorish, and Renaissance architecture. The palace features an array of towers, turrets, and domes, as well as decorative features such as gargoyles, sculptures, and colorful tiles.

Inside, the palace is equally impressive, with ornate furnishings, intricate carvings, and intricate tilework. Visitors can explore the palace's various rooms, including the King's and Queen's apartments, the music room, the chapel, and the dining room.

One of the highlights of a visit to Pena Palace is the panoramic views from its terraces and balconies. From here, visitors can take in sweeping views of Sintra's lush forests and rolling hills, as well as the Atlantic Ocean in the distance.

Overall, Pena Palace is a must-visit destination for anyone traveling to Portugal, offering a unique and unforgettable experience for history buffs, architecture enthusiasts, and nature lovers alike.

Here are some additional interesting facts and information about Pena Palace:

Pena Palace was built on the ruins of an old monastery, which had been damaged in a fire in the 18th century. Some of the monastery's structures, such as the cloister, were incorporated into the new palace.

The palace's vibrant colors were not added until the 20th century. In the 1990s, the palace underwent a major restoration project that restored the original colors and decorative elements of the palace's facade.

The palace's interior is decorated with a mix of styles, including neo-Gothic, neo-Manueline, and Moorish-inspired elements. This eclectic style was typical of the Romanticist period, which valued individualism and creativity over strict adherence to tradition.

The palace's park covers over 200 hectares and includes a variety of landscapes, from dense forests to landscaped gardens. The park is home to a wide variety of plant and animal species, including several rare and endangered species.

The palace is located on the top of a hill, which can be reached by a steep uphill walk or by taking a bus or taxi. Visitors can also take a guided tour of the palace and park, which provides additional information about the palace's history and architecture.

Pena Palace is a UNESCO World Heritage Site and is considered one of the finest examples of Romanticist architecture in Europe. It has been featured in numerous films and television shows, including "The Night Manager" and "Amazing Race."

MOORISH CASTLE

The Moorish Castle is a historical fortress located in Sintra, Portugal. It was built in the 8th and 9th centuries by the Moors, who occupied the Iberian Peninsula for several centuries. The castle served as a military stronghold and provided protection for the surrounding area.

The castle consists of two main sections: the upper and lower castles. The upper castle is the oldest part of the fortress, and it includes a cistern, towers, and walls. The lower castle was built later, in the 12th century, and includes a palace, chapel, and other buildings.

In the 12th century, after the Christian reconquest of Portugal, the castle was taken over by the Portuguese army. Over the centuries, it fell into disrepair, but in the 19th century, it was restored and became a popular tourist attraction.

Today, the Moorish Castle is a UNESCO World Heritage Site and is visited by thousands of tourists every year. It offers stunning views of the surrounding landscape and provides visitors with a glimpse into Portugal's rich history.

QUINTA DA REGALEIRA

Quinta da Regaleira is a historic estate located in the town of Sintra, Portugal. The estate was built between 1904 and 1910 by the wealthy Portuguese businessman António Augusto Carvalho Monteiro, in collaboration with the Italian architect Luigi Manini. The estate is known for its ornate palace, chapel, gardens, and underground tunnels.

The palace features Gothic, Renaissance, and Manueline architectural styles, and is decorated with intricate carvings, sculptures, and stained-glass windows. The chapel is dedicated to Our Lady of the Regaleira and features murals depicting scenes from the life of Christ.

The gardens are a mix of formal and natural elements, featuring fountains, terraces, lakes, grottoes, and a variety of plants and trees. The highlight of the garden is the Initiation Well, a deep, spiral staircase that leads down to a subterranean chamber.

The underground tunnels at Quinta da Regaleira were used for secretive rituals and initiations by Monteiro, who was a member of the Rosicrucian Order. The tunnels connect various parts of the estate, including the palace, chapel, and gardens.

Today, Quinta da Regaleira is a popular tourist attraction and is recognized as a UNESCO World Heritage Site. Visitors can explore the palace, chapel, gardens, and underground tunnels, and learn about the history and symbolism of the estate.

SINTRA-CASCAIS NATURAL PARK

Sintra-Cascais Natural Park is a protected area located in the Lisbon District of Portugal. It covers an area of approximately 145 square kilometers and is known for its diverse landscape and rich cultural heritage. The natural park encompasses the Serra de Sintra mountain range, which is a popular tourist destination and home to several historical sites and monuments.

The park is home to a wide variety of flora and fauna, including cork oaks, chestnut trees, and numerous bird species. The area is also home to several beautiful beaches, such as Guincho Beach, which is known for its excellent surfing conditions.

One of the main attractions of the park is the town of Sintra, which is a UNESCO World Heritage site and is famous for its stunning palaces and castles, such as the Pena Palace and the Castle of the Moors. Another popular attraction is Cabo da Roca, which is the westernmost point of mainland Europe and offers spectacular views of the Atlantic Ocean.

Overall, the Sintra-Cascais Natural Park is a unique and beautiful area that offers visitors a combination of natural beauty and cultural richness. Whether you're interested in hiking, history, or simply enjoying the outdoors, this park is definitely worth a visit.

ALGARVE

The Algarve is a region located in the southernmost part of Portugal. It is known for its beautiful beaches, warm climate, and scenic countryside. The region covers an area of approximately 5,400 square kilometers and is bordered by the Atlantic Ocean to the south and west. The Algarve is divided into 16 municipalities, with Faro being the largest and most populous.

The Algarve has a long history, with evidence of human settlement dating back to prehistoric times. The region was occupied by various civilizations over the centuries, including the Romans, Moors, and Christians. Today, the Algarve is a popular tourist destination, attracting millions of visitors each year. It is renowned for its picturesque coastal towns and villages, as well as its many golf courses, water parks, and other recreational facilities.

The region is also famous for its seafood dishes, such as grilled sardines, clams, and octopus, which are served in many of the local restaurants. Other popular dishes include cataplana, a seafood stew cooked in a copper pot, and arroz de marisco, a rice dish with shellfish.

The Algarve is easily accessible by air, with Faro International Airport serving as the main gateway. There are also several major highways and motorways that connect the region to other parts of Portugal and Spain

LAGOS

Lagos is a historic town located in the Algarve region of Portugal. It is situated on the western side of the region, and it is one of the most popular tourist destinations in the Algarve. Lagos is known for its picturesque old town, stunning beaches, and rich history, making it an ideal destination for travelers looking for a mix of culture, natural beauty, and recreation.

One of the most notable landmarks in Lagos is the ancient city walls, which date back to the 16th century. These walls were built to protect the town from pirate attacks and other invasions, and they offer a glimpse into the town's past. Other historical landmarks in Lagos include the Church of St. Anthony, the Governor's Castle, and the 17th-century Santo Antonio Church.

Lagos is also known for its beautiful beaches, which are some of the best in the Algarve. One of the most popular is Praia Dona Ana, a secluded cove with crystal-clear waters and golden sand. Other popular beaches in Lagos include Meia Praia, Praia do Camilo, and Praia da Batata, which offer a range of water sports and other recreational activities.

In addition to its natural beauty and historic landmarks, Lagos is also renowned for its vibrant nightlife. The town has a bustling bar and restaurant scene, with many options to choose from. Visitors can sample local specialties such as grilled sardines, seafood stews, and traditional Portuguese desserts, such as pastel de nata.
Overall, Lagos is a charming and picturesque town that offers something for everyone. Its rich history, stunning beaches, and lively nightlife make it an ideal destination for travelers looking to experience the best of the Algarve region.

PRAIA DA ROCHA

Praia da Rocha is a popular beach resort town located in the Algarve region of southern Portugal. The town is known for its stunning beaches, dramatic cliffs, and lively nightlife.

The beach at Praia da Rocha is a long stretch of golden sand that is backed by towering cliffs. The beach is ideal for swimming, sunbathing, and water sports, and there are plenty of amenities available including restaurants, cafes, and bars.

In addition to the beach, Praia da Rocha has a lively nightlife scene with numerous bars, clubs, and discos. The town also has a casino and a range of other entertainment options.

Praia da Rocha is located just a few kilometers from the city of Portimão, which is the largest town in the western Algarve. Portimão has a range of shops, restaurants, and cultural attractions, including the Museum of Portimão and the Church of Our Lady of Conception.

Praia da Rocha is a great destination for anyone looking to enjoy a beach vacation with plenty of amenities and entertainment options.

TAVIRA

Tavira is a city in the Algarve region of Portugal. It is located on the eastern side of the Algarve, close to the Spanish border. Tavira is known for its historic center, which is full of charming cobbled streets, traditional white-washed houses, and historic churches. One of the most notable attractions in Tavira is the Roman bridge that spans the Gilão River and connects the two sides of the city. The city is also home to several museums, including the Tavira Municipal Museum, which showcases the region's rich history and culture. Additionally, Tavira is known for its beautiful beaches, which are popular with tourists during the summer months. Overall, Tavira is a lovely destination for those looking to experience Portugal's history and culture, as well as its stunning natural scenery.

CABO DE SÃO VICENTE

Cabo de São Vicente, also known as Cape St. Vincent, is a headland located in the southwestern tip of Portugal, in the Algarve region. It is the most southwestern point of mainland Europe and has been an important landmark for sailors for centuries.

The cape is named after Saint Vincent of Saragossa, a Christian martyr who is the patron saint of Lisbon. The area around the cape has a rich history and has been inhabited since prehistoric times. The Phoenicians, Romans, and Moors all left their mark on the region, and the cape was an important site during the Age of Discovery, as it was a starting point for many exploratory voyages.

Today, the area around Cape St. Vincent is a popular tourist destination, known for its stunning views of the Atlantic Ocean and rugged coastline. The cape is home to a lighthouse, which was built in the 19th century and is still in operation today. There are also several hiking trails in the area, which offer visitors the opportunity to explore the natural beauty of the region.

Chapter 4

Food and Drink

TRADITIONAL PORTUGUESE DISHES

Portugal has a rich culinary tradition with a wide variety of dishes. Here are some traditional Portuguese dishes:

Bacalhau à Gomes de Sá - A dish made with salt cod, potatoes, onions, and olives, cooked in the oven with eggs and parsley.

Cozido à Portuguesa - A hearty stew made with a variety of meats, including beef, pork, chicken, and sometimes chorizo sausage, along with beans, potatoes, cabbage, and carrots.

Caldo Verde - A soup made with potatoes, kale, and sometimes chorizo sausage, served with cornbread or crusty bread.

Francesinha - A sandwich made with ham, linguiça sausage, and steak, topped with melted cheese and a tomato-based sauce, often served with fries.

Arroz de Pato - A duck and rice casserole, flavored with olives, chorizo sausage, and often topped with a fried egg.

Leitão à Bairrada - Roast suckling pig, seasoned with garlic, salt, and pepper, often served with roasted potatoes and a salad.

Polvo à Lagareiro - Octopus grilled with olive oil, garlic, and herbs, often served with roasted potatoes.

Açorda - A bread soup made with garlic, olive oil, and cilantro, often served with shrimp or cod.

Sardinhas Assadas - Grilled sardines, often served with roasted potatoes and a salad.

Bolo do Caco - A type of bread made with sweet potato and served with garlic butter. These are just a few of the many delicious traditional Portuguese dishes you should tryout.

PORTUGUESE FOOD RANKED

www.tasteatlas.com/portugal

BEST ★ 4.5+
- PASTEL DE NATA — 4.7
- AMÊIJOAS À BULHÃO PATO — 4.7
- ESPETADA — 4.5

GREAT ★ 4.0+
- FEIJOADA À PORTUGUESA — 4.4
- POLVO À LAGAREIRO — 4.3
- FRANCESINHA — 4.0

OK ★ 3.5+
- COZIDO — 3.8
- CALDEIRADA — 3.8
- CHANFANA — 3.7

WORST ★ <3.5
- BOLO REI — 2.9
- TRIPAS À MODA DO PORTO — 3.0
- MEIA-DESFEITA — 3.4

WINE REGIONS AND VARIETALS

Portugal is home to many wine regions, each with its own unique characteristics and grape varietals. Here are some of the most important wine regions and grape varietals in Portugal:

Douro: The Douro Valley is located in the north of Portugal and is one of the oldest wine regions in the world. The main grape varietals used in Douro wines are Touriga Nacional, Touriga Franca, Tinta Roriz, and Tinta Barroca. The wines from this region are typically full-bodied and rich.

Alentejo: Alentejo is located in the south of Portugal and is known for producing high-quality red wines. The main grape varietals used in Alentejo wines are Aragonês (also known as Tempranillo), Trincadeira, and Alicante Bouschet. The wines from this region are typically full-bodied with intense flavors.

Vinho Verde: Vinho Verde is a wine region located in the northwest of Portugal. The main grape varietals used in Vinho Verde wines are Loureiro, Alvarinho, and Trajadura. The wines from this region are known for their crisp acidity and light body.

Dão: The Dão wine region is located in the center of Portugal. The main grape varietals used in Dão wines are Touriga Nacional, Tinta Roriz, and Jaen. The wines from this region are typically full-bodied with intense flavors.

Bairrada: Bairrada is located in the northwest of Portugal. The main grape varietals used in Bairrada wines are Baga, Touriga Nacional, and Tinta Barroca. The wines from this region are known for their tannic structure and complex flavors.

Other notable grape varietals in Portugal include Castelão, Bical, Encruzado, and Arinto. In addition to these grape varieties, Portugal is also known for its fortified wines, such as Port and Madeira.

PORTO TASTING

Porto, also known as port wine, is a fortified wine that is produced exclusively in the Douro Valley in northern Portugal. It is typically a sweet red wine that is fortified with a neutral grape spirit, which stops fermentation and leaves residual sugar in the wine.

A Porto tasting typically involves trying a range of different port wines, including different styles and vintages. Some of the most common styles of port wine include:

Tawny port: This style of port is aged in oak barrels, which imparts a nutty, caramel flavor to the wine. Tawny ports are typically lighter in color and have a smoother, more mellow taste than other styles.

Ruby port: This style of port is aged in stainless steel tanks, which preserves its bright red color and fruity flavor. Ruby ports are typically full-bodied and have a more pronounced fruit flavor than other styles.

Vintage port: This is the most prestigious and expensive style of port wine. Vintage ports are made only in exceptional years and are aged in the bottle, rather than in barrels. They are known for their complex flavor profiles, which can include notes of dark fruit, chocolate, and spice.

When tasting port wine, it's important to consider the wine's appearance, aroma, flavor, and finish. Some of the key characteristics to look for include:

- Appearance: Is the wine clear or cloudy? What is its color?
- Aroma: What do you smell when you swirl the wine in the glass? Are there any notes of fruit, spice, or oak?
- Flavor: What flavors do you taste when you take a sip? Is the wine sweet or dry? Is it fruity or more earthy?

- Finish: How long does the flavor of the wine linger after you swallow? Is it a pleasant or unpleasant aftertaste?

When pairing port wine with food, it's important to consider the wine's sweetness and intensity. Tawny ports are often paired with desserts like fruit tarts or nutty cheeses, while ruby ports are a good match for chocolate or strong cheeses. Vintage ports are often enjoyed on their own or paired with rich, savory dishes like game meats or stews..

Chapter 5

CULTURE AND HISTORY

FADO MUSIC AND CULTURE

Fado is a traditional genre of Portuguese music that dates back to the early 19th century. It is often characterized by mournful and soulful singing, accompanied by the Portuguese guitar and sometimes other instruments. Fado is often associated with feelings of saudade, a Portuguese word that refers to a deep longing or nostalgia for something or someone that is lost.

Fado is believed to have originated in the port city of Lisbon, where it was performed in the city's taverns and cafes by sailors, prostitutes, and other working-class people. Over time, fado became more widely popular and was embraced by Portugal's middle and upper classes.

In 2011, fado was recognized by UNESCO as an Intangible Cultural Heritage of Humanity, which has helped to raise its profile around the world. Today, fado is performed in many countries, including Brazil, Argentina, and the United States, but it remains most closely associated with Portugal.

In addition to its music, fado is also associated with a particular culture and way of life. Fado performances often take place in intimate venues, such as small bars or cafes, and are typically accompanied by food and drink. The culture of fado is also closely tied to the Portuguese concept of saudade, which emphasizes a sense of melancholy and nostalgia for the past.

Overall, fado is a rich and complex genre of music that reflects the history and culture of Portugal. Its popularity around the world is a testament to its enduring appeal and its ability to connect with people on a deep emotional level.

HISTORY

Fado originated in the early 19th century in Lisbon, Portugal, but its exact origins are unclear. Some historians believe that it was influenced by Arabic music, while others believe that it was inspired by the traditional music of rural Portugal. In any case, fado was initially performed by sailors, prostitutes, and other working-class people in the city's taverns and cafes.

Over time, fado became more widely popular and began to be performed by professional musicians in theaters and other venues. In the mid-20th century, fado enjoyed a revival, thanks in part to the popularity of fado singer Amália Rodrigues, who became known as the "Queen of Fado".

MUSIC

Fado music is characterized by its mournful and soulful singing style, often accompanied by the Portuguese guitar, a pear-shaped instrument with twelve strings, and sometimes a classical guitar or a bass guitar. The lyrics of fado songs often deal with themes of love, loss, and longing, and are typically sung in a slow, emotive style.

There are two main types of fado: fado de Lisboa, which is associated with Lisbon and tends to be more traditional and melancholic, and fado de Coimbra, which is associated with the university town of Coimbra and is often more upbeat and academic in nature.

CULTURE

Fado is closely associated with Portuguese culture and is often performed in small, intimate venues such as bars and cafes. These venues are sometimes referred to as fado houses or fado restaurants, and they often serve traditional Portuguese cuisine and wine.

The culture of fado is also closely tied to the concept of saudade, a Portuguese word that refers to a deep sense of longing or nostalgia. Saudade is an important part of Portuguese culture and is reflected in the melancholic lyrics and emotive singing style of fado music.

Today, fado remains an important part of Portuguese culture and is celebrated at events such as the annual Fado Festival in Lisbon. It has also gained a following around the world, with fado clubs and festivals in cities such as New York, Paris, and Tokyo.

MUSEUMS AND ART GALLERIES

There are many museums and art galleries to visit in Portugal, showcasing the country's rich cultural heritage and contemporary artistic expression. Here are some notable ones to explore:

National Museum of Ancient Art (Lisbon) - This museum houses a vast collection of Portuguese art, including painting, sculpture, and decorative arts, from the Middle Ages to the 19th century.

Calouste Gulbenkian Museum (Lisbon) - The Gulbenkian Museum displays an impressive collection of art from around the world, including European paintings, Islamic art, and East Asian ceramics.

Museum of Contemporary Art of Serralves (Porto) - This museum showcases contemporary art from Portugal and around the world, with a focus on the intersection of art, architecture, and landscape design.

Berardo Collection Museum (Lisbon) - The Berardo Collection Museum is home to an extensive collection of modern and contemporary art, featuring works by artists such as Pablo Picasso, Salvador Dalí, and Andy Warhol.

National Tile Museum (Lisbon) - The National Tile Museum explores the history and significance of Portuguese tilework, with a collection spanning from the 15th century to the present day.

Chiado Museum (Lisbon) - The Chiado Museum is located in a historic building in the heart of Lisbon's Chiado neighborhood, and features a collection of Portuguese art from the 19th and 20th centuries.

Casa da Música (Porto) - While not a traditional art museum, Casa da Música is a stunning concert hall designed by renowned architect Rem Koolhaas, and is a must-visit destination for architecture and music enthusiasts alike.

These are just a few examples of the many museums and art galleries to explore in Portugal. Whether you're interested in ancient art, contemporary exhibitions, or cultural heritage, there is something for everyone to discover

HISTORICAL SITES AND LANDMARKS

1). Jeronimos Monastery: Located in Lisbon, the Jeronimos Monastery is a UNESCO World Heritage Site and one of the most impressive examples of Manueline architecture in Portugal.

2). Tower of Belem: Also located in Lisbon, the Tower of Belem is another UNESCO World Heritage Site and a symbol of Portugal's Age of Discovery.

3). Convent of Christ: Situated in Tomar, the Convent of Christ is a medieval castle and a UNESCO World Heritage Site.

4). Pena Palace: Located in Sintra, the Pena Palace is a colorful and eccentric palace built in the 19th century.

5). Alcobaça Monastery: A Cistercian monastery located in the town of Alcobaça, this site is also a UNESCO World Heritage Site.

6). Castle of Guimarães: Located in the city of Guimarães, this castle is considered the birthplace of Portugal and is a UNESCO World Heritage Site.

7). Roman Temple of Évora: Located in Évora, this Roman temple is one of the best-preserved Roman structures in Portugal and a UNESCO World Heritage Site.

8). University of Coimbra: Founded in 1290, the University of Coimbra is one of the oldest universities in Europe and a UNESCO World Heritage Site.

9). Capela dos Ossos: Located in Évora, the Capela dos Ossos (Chapel of Bones) is a small chapel decorated with human bones and skulls.

10). Palace of Mafra: Located in Mafra, the Palace of Mafra is a Baroque palace and a UNESCO World Heritage Site.
Quinta da Regaleira: A beautiful estate and garden located in Sintra, the Quinta da Regaleira features a palace, chapel, and a unique network of underground tunnels and caves.

11). Batalha Monastery: A Gothic-style monastery located in the town of Batalha, this site is also a UNESCO World Heritage Site.

12). National Palace of Sintra: A medieval palace located in Sintra, this site was used as a royal residence from the 13th to the 19th centuries.

13). Ribeira Palace: A former royal palace located in Lisbon, the Ribeira Palace was destroyed in the 18th century by an earthquake, but its ruins can still be visited today.

14). Castle of Almourol: Located on a small island in the Tagus River, the Castle of Almourol is a medieval castle that dates back to the 12th century.

15). Sanctuary of Our Lady of Fatima: A major Catholic pilgrimage site located in Fatima, the Sanctuary of Our Lady of Fatima attracts millions of visitors each year.

16). Palace of the Dukes of Braganza: Located in Guimarães, this palace was once the residence of the Dukes of Braganza and is now a museum.

17). Monastery of Santa Clara-a-Velha: Located in Coimbra, this medieval monastery was abandoned for centuries and only rediscovered in the 20th century.

18). Castle of the Moors: A medieval castle located in Sintra, the Castle of the Moors offers stunning views of the surrounding countryside.

19). Vasco da Gama Bridge: A modern landmark located in Lisbon, the Vasco da Gama Bridge is one of the longest bridges in Europe and an impressive feat of engineering

Chapter 6

OUTDOOR ACTIVITIES

SURFING AND BEACHES

Portugal is a popular destination for surfing and beach lovers. With over 800 km of coastline, there are plenty of beaches and surf spots to choose from. Here are some of the best beaches and surf spots in Portugal:

Peniche - Located on the west coast of Portugal, Peniche is known for its consistent surf breaks and hosts the annual Rip Curl Pro Portugal competition. The beach town has plenty of surf schools and accommodations for surfers.

Nazaré - Nazaré is home to some of the biggest waves in the world, with surfers coming from all over to ride its famous waves. The town has a variety of surf spots for all levels, and is a great place to watch the pros tackle the massive waves.

Ericeira - A World Surf Reserve since 2011, Ericeira is a popular spot for surfers of all levels. With a variety of surf breaks, including some of the best point breaks in Europe, Ericeira is a great place to improve your skills.

Praia do Norte - Another big wave spot, Praia do Norte is located in Nazaré and is known for its massive waves that can reach up to 100 feet. It's definitely not for beginners, but experienced surfers will find some of the most challenging waves in the world here.

Costa da Caparica - Just a short drive from Lisbon, Costa da Caparica has over 20 km of sandy beaches and plenty of surf schools. It's a popular spot for locals and tourists alike, and has a variety of surf breaks for all levels.

Portugal has a great surf culture and is a top destination for surfers from around the world. Whether you're a beginner or an experienced surfer, there's a surf spot in Portugal that's perfect for you.

HIKING AND NATURE RESERVES

Portugal offers a variety of hiking trails and nature reserves for outdoor enthusiasts. Here are some popular destinations:

Peneda-Gerês National Park - Located in the northern part of Portugal, this park is known for its stunning scenery, including waterfalls, rivers, and mountain peaks. The park offers a variety of hiking trails for all skill levels.

Ria Formosa Natural Park - This park is located in the southern part of Portugal, and is a popular destination for bird watching and hiking. The park's trails take you through salt pans, wetlands, and coastal lagoons.

Serra da Estrela Natural Park - This park is located in central Portugal, and is home to the highest mountain range in mainland Portugal. The park offers hiking trails that take you through valleys, forests, and granite peaks.

Sintra-Cascais Natural Park - This park is located just outside of Lisbon, and is known for its beautiful coastline and dense forests. The park offers hiking trails that take you through historic castles, palaces, and gardens.

Faial Island - This island is located in the Azores archipelago, and is known for its volcanic landscapes, including a massive crater known as the Caldeira. The island offers hiking trails that take you through forests and lava fields.

These are just a few of the many hiking destinations and nature reserves in Portugal. Whether you're a seasoned hiker or just starting out, Portugal has something to offer for everyone who loves the outdoors

CYCLING TOURS

Portugal is a fantastic destination for cycling tours, with its diverse landscapes, stunning coastlines, historic cities, and charming villages. Here are some popular cycling tours in Portugal:

The Alentejo Wine Route: This tour takes you through the beautiful countryside of Alentejo, known for its vineyards and wine production. You'll visit traditional villages and historic towns, cycle along scenic routes, and enjoy delicious local cuisine.

The Atlantic Coast: This tour follows the coastline from Porto to Lisbon, passing through charming fishing villages, sandy beaches, and beautiful natural parks. You'll also have the opportunity to visit historic sites such as the castle of Óbidos and the Sanctuary of Fátima.

The Douro Valley: This tour takes you through the Douro Valley, one of the oldest wine regions in the world and a UNESCO World Heritage Site. You'll cycle through vineyards and along the Douro River, enjoying stunning views of the valley and tasting delicious local wines.

The Azores Islands: This tour takes you to the beautiful islands of the Azores, where you'll cycle through lush green landscapes, volcanic craters, and beautiful coastal routes. You'll also have the opportunity to go whale watching and visit hot springs and natural pools.

The Camino de Santiago: This tour follows the Camino de Santiago, a historic pilgrimage route that ends in Santiago de Compostela in Spain. You'll cycle through beautiful landscapes and historic towns, meeting fellow pilgrims along the way and experiencing the unique culture and traditions of the region.

These are just a few examples of the many cycling tours available in Portugal. Whether you're a seasoned cyclist or a beginner, there's a tour to suit your interests and abilities

Chapter 7

PRACTICAL INFORMATION

ACCOMMODATION OPTIONS

When traveling to Portugal, there are various accommodation options to choose from depending on your preferences and budget. Some of the most popular options include:

Hotels: There are plenty of hotels in Portugal ranging from budget-friendly to luxury ones. You can choose from chain hotels, boutique hotels, or traditional Portuguese hotels. You can use online booking platforms like Booking.com, Agoda.com or Expedia.com to find suitable hotels in Portugal.

Hostels: If you're a budget traveler or a solo traveler, hostels are a great option for you. Portugal has numerous hostels in major cities and tourist destinations. Hostels offer dormitory-style rooms and private rooms at affordable prices. Popular websites to book hostels in Portugal include Hostelworld.com and Hostels.com.

Guesthouses: Guesthouses are smaller accommodations that are typically run by families. They offer a more homely and traditional feel compared to hotels. Guesthouses usually have fewer rooms and provide personalized service. You can book guesthouses through websites like Booking.com and Airbnb.

Apartments: Renting an apartment is a great option if you're traveling with family or friends or if you're planning a long-term stay in Portugal. You can choose from studio apartments to large apartments with multiple rooms. Websites like Airbnb, Booking.com, and HomeAway offer a wide range of apartments for rent in Portugal.

Villas: If you're traveling with a larger group of friends or family, renting a villa can be a great option. Villas offer more space, privacy, and amenities compared to hotels or apartments. Websites like Airbnb, HomeAway, and Luxury Retreats offer a range of villas in Portugal.

Portugal has a range of accommodation options to suit all budgets and preferences. It's recommended to book your accommodation in advance, especially during peak tourist seasons, to avoid disappointment.

Here are a few more accommodation options when traveling to Portugal:

Pousadas: Pousadas are historic buildings that have been converted into luxury hotels. They offer a unique and authentic experience of Portugal's rich history and culture. Pousadas can be found in historic towns and cities across the country, such as Lisbon, Porto, and Evora. You can book Pousadas through the official website of Pestana Pousadas.

Camping: If you enjoy the outdoors and nature, camping can be a great option when traveling to Portugal. The country has numerous campsites, many of which are located near beaches and national parks. You can either bring your own camping gear or rent equipment from the campsite. Popular camping websites in Portugal include Orbitur and Campingred.

Rural Tourism: Rural tourism is a unique and popular way to experience the Portuguese countryside. This type of accommodation offers a peaceful and authentic experience in traditional farmhouses, cottages, and manor houses. You can book rural tourism stays through the official website of the Portuguese Tourism Board.

Boat Accommodation: If you're looking for a unique experience, consider booking boat accommodation in Portugal. You can rent a boat and sleep on board, or book a room on a yacht or a houseboat. There are many marinas and ports across the country that offer boat accommodation. Websites like Airbnb and Book a Boat offer a variety of boat accommodation options in Portugal.

These are just a few of the accommodation options available when traveling to Portugal. Whether you're looking for luxury or budget-friendly options, there's something for everyone in this beautiful country.

LOCAL TRANSPORTATION

Portugal has a well-developed public transportation system, and there are various options for local transportation within the country.

Bus: Buses are the most common mode of public transportation in Portugal. They are available in all major cities and towns and are relatively inexpensive. The major bus operators in Portugal are Rede Expressos, Rodoviária Nacional, and Transdev.

Tram: Trams are a popular mode of transportation in Lisbon and Porto. In Lisbon, the tram network covers most of the city, and the iconic yellow trams are a popular tourist attraction. In Porto, the tram system is smaller but still an efficient way to get around the city.

Metro: Lisbon and Porto have efficient and well-connected metro systems that cover most of the city. The metro in Lisbon is the oldest in the country and has four lines, while the metro in Porto has six lines.

Train: Portugal has an extensive train network that connects all major cities and towns. The trains are fast, comfortable, and affordable. The two main train operators in Portugal are CP (Comboios de Portugal) and Fertagus.

Taxis: Taxis are widely available in all major cities and towns in Portugal. They are metered, and the fares are reasonable. However, be aware that taxi fares can be higher at night, on weekends, and during holidays.

Car Rental: Renting a car is a good option if you plan to explore rural areas or smaller towns. The major car rental companies in Portugal are Hertz, Avis, Europcar, and Budget.

Overall, Portugal has a reliable and efficient public transportation system, and you can easily get around the country using a combination of buses, trams, metros, and trains

LANGUAGE AND CUSTOMS

Portuguese is the official language of Portugal, and it is spoken by nearly all of the population. In addition to Portuguese, there are several regional dialects and minority languages spoken in the country, including Mirandese, which has official recognition in some municipalities of northeastern Portugal.

Portuguese culture is heavily influenced by its history as a colonial power, as well as by its proximity to other European countries. Some traditional customs and practices in Portugal include:

Fado: This is a type of music that is unique to Portugal, and it is characterized by mournful and soulful melodies. It is often sung in small, intimate settings like cafes or restaurants.

Food and wine: Portugal is known for its delicious seafood dishes, as well as for its wine, particularly Port wine. Some popular Portuguese dishes include bacalhau (salt cod), cozido (a hearty stew), and pastéis de nata (custard tarts).

Festivals: Portugal has many festivals throughout the year, including Carnival, Easter, and Saint Anthony's Day, which is celebrated with street parties and traditional food.

Religious traditions: Portugal is predominantly Catholic, and many of its customs and traditions are tied to the Catholic faith. This includes the observance of Holy Week, the celebration of the Feast of the Assumption, and the lighting of candles in churches.

Family values: Family is highly valued in Portuguese culture, and there is a strong emphasis on respect for elders and close family ties. Many families still live in multi-generational households, and it is common for people to have large extended families.

Portugal has a rich and diverse culture that is deeply rooted in its history and traditions.

Basic Portuguese languages that tourists should know.
If you're planning to visit Portugal, here are some basic Portuguese phrases that can be helpful:

Hello - Olá
Goodbye - Adeus
Please - Por favor
Thank you - Obrigado (if you're male), Obrigada (if you're female)
Yes - Sim
No - Não
Excuse me - Desculpe
Sorry - Desculpe
Do you speak English? - Fala inglês?
I don't understand - Não percebo
How much does it cost? - Quanto custa?
Where is...? - Onde fica...?
Can you help me? - Pode ajudar-me?
I would like... - Eu gostaria...
Cheers! - Saúde!

Learning a few basic phrases in Portuguese can make your trip to Portugal more enjoyable and help you connect with the local people

TRAVEL TIPS AND SAFETY PRECAUTIONS

Explore the cities: Portugal has many beautiful cities, including Lisbon, Porto, Coimbra, and Faro. Each has its own unique charm and history, so take the time to explore them all.

Learn some Portuguese: While many Portuguese people speak English, it's always helpful to know some basic phrases in Portuguese. This can help you navigate and communicate with locals more easily.

Try the local cuisine: Portugal has a rich culinary tradition, so make sure to try some of the local specialties, like bacalhau (salt cod), pastéis de nata (custard tarts), and port wine.

Take a day trip: Portugal is a small country, so it's easy to take a day trip to nearby towns or villages. Some popular destinations include Sintra, Évora, and the Douro Valley.

Be aware of pickpockets: Like in many tourist destinations, pickpocketing can be a problem in Portugal. Be aware of your surroundings and keep your belongings close to you.

Visit the beaches: Portugal has some of the most beautiful beaches in Europe, so take some time to relax and soak up the sun.

Respect the culture: Portugal has a rich history and culture, so be respectful of its traditions and customs. Dress modestly when visiting churches and other religious sites.

Use public transportation: Portugal has a good public transportation system, so consider taking buses or trains to get around. This can be cheaper and more convenient than renting a car.

Plan ahead: Portugal is a popular tourist destination, especially during the summer months, so it's a good idea to plan ahead and book accommodations and activities in advance.

Enjoy the nightlife: Portugal has a vibrant nightlife scene, especially in Lisbon and Porto. Take advantage of the local bars, clubs, and live music venues.
Portugal is a beautiful and diverse country with so much to offer tourists. From its vibrant cities and stunning beaches to its rich history and culture, there is something for everyone to enjoy. By following these travel tips, you can make the most of your trip and have an unforgettable experience in Portugal. So pack your bags, brush up on your Portuguese, and get ready to discover all that this incredible country has to offer

CONCLUSION

In conclusion, Portugal is a beautiful and diverse country that offers travelers a wide range of experiences. From its stunning coastline and beaches to its vibrant cities and rich cultural heritage, there is something for everyone to enjoy.

One of the highlights of Portugal is its warm and welcoming people, who are always ready to share their culture and traditions with visitors. This is reflected in the country's food, which is a fusion of traditional Mediterranean and Atlantic flavors, and its wine, which is world-renowned for its quality and diversity.

For those looking to explore Portugal's natural beauty, there are many options, including hiking in the mountains or along the coastline, surfing in the Atlantic, or visiting the country's many national parks.

Portugal's cities are also worth exploring, with Lisbon and Porto being the most popular destinations. Lisbon, the capital, is known for its stunning architecture, charming streets, and vibrant nightlife. Porto, on the other hand, is famous for its historic center, where visitors can sample the city's famous port wine and enjoy the picturesque riverside scenery.

Overall, Portugal is a destination that should not be missed by any traveler seeking a unique and unforgettable experience. Its combination of natural beauty, cultural heritage, delicious food and wine, and friendly people make it a truly special place to visit.

RESOURCES FOR FURTHER INFORMATION

Here are some resources you can use to gather more information on traveling to Portugal:

Visit Portugal: This is the official tourism website of Portugal. It provides comprehensive information on the country's history, culture, food, accommodations, transportation, and activities.

Lonely Planet: This travel guidebook company provides detailed information on Portugal's top destinations, attractions, and activities. They also offer practical travel tips and advice.

Rick Steves' Europe: This popular travel show and website features detailed information on Portugal, including travel guides, recommended itineraries, and cultural insights.

Rough Guides: This travel guidebook company provides comprehensive information on Portugal's history, culture, food, accommodations, transportation, and activities.

Fodor's Travel: This travel guidebook company provides comprehensive information on Portugal's top destinations, attractions, and activities. They also offer practical travel tips and advice.

Portugalist: This is a travel blog that provides practical information and insider tips on traveling to Portugal. It covers everything from food and drink to accommodations and transportation.

Culture Trip: This online travel guide provides information on Portugal's history, culture, food, accommodations, transportation, and activities. It also features articles written by locals that offer insider tips on where to go and what to see.

Tripadvisor: This website provides reviews and ratings of hotels, restaurants, and attractions in Portugal. It's a great resource for finding the best places to stay, eat, and visit.

Expedia: This travel booking website provides information on flights, hotels, and vacation packages to Portugal. It also offers customer reviews and ratings to help you make informed decisions.

Airbnb: This website provides a wide variety of accommodations in Portugal, from apartments to villas to unique and quirky homes. It's a great option for travelers who want to experience local life and culture.

PORTUGAL MAP

Printed in Great Britain
by Amazon